MW00626455

Clare Lizzimore

ANIMAL

Productions in Print

An In An Hour Book
www.inanhourbooks.com
An imprint of Smith and Kraus Publishers, Inc.
Published by Smith and Kraus, Inc.
177 Lyme Road, Hanover, NH 03755
www.SmithandKraus.com

Animal
by
Clare Lizzimore

Copyright © 2015 by Clare Lizzimore.
All rights reserved.

CAUTION: Professionals and amateurs are hereby warned that any performance of *Animal* is subject to the payment of a royalty. It is fully protected under the copyright laws of the United States of America and of all countries covered by the International Copyright Union (including the Dominion of Canada and the rest of the British Commonwealth.), the Berne Convention, the Pan-American Copyright Convention, and the Universal Copyright Convention, as well as all countries with which the United States has reciprocal copyright relations. All rights, including professional / amateur stage rights, motion picture, recitation, lecturing, public reading, radio broadcasting, television, video or sound recording, all other forms of mechanical, digital or electronic reproduction, transmission, exhibition and distribution, such as CD, DVD, the Internet, private and file-sharing networks, information storage and retrieval systems and photocopying, and the rights of translation into foreign languages, are strictly reserved. Particular emphasis is laid upon the matter of readings, permission for which must be secured from the Author's agent in writing.

ALL INQUIRIES CONCERNING RIGHTS, INCLUDING AMATEUR STAGE RIGHTS, SHOULD BE ADDRESSED TO: CASAROTTO RAMSAY & ASSOCIATES LIMITED, WAVERLEY HOUSE 7-12 NOEL STREET LONDON W1F 8GQ. ATTN: RACHEL TAYLOR

Manufactured in the United States of America, September 2015.

Cover Design: Shawn Helm
Interior Layout: Adrien-Alice Hansel

Studio Theatre presents

Animal

Clare Lizzimore

first performance September 30, 2015

Introduction

As I write this, we're about two weeks away from *Animal*'s opening. Since it is very much a work in development, I'm not sure exactly what play you'll be reading. That's part of the thrill of new project development, especially when you're a theatre that believes that plays are found as much in rehearsal and production as at a writer's desk.

What I do know is that Clare Lizzimore, a director who has turned some of her attentions to writing, has a vivid theatrical imagination, a direct and economical writing style that leaves room for a kind of everyday poetry, and a refreshing boldness when it comes to revisions and rewrites. It has been a thrill to watch how her kernel of an idea about a particular brand of psychic distress became this meditation on marriage, disconnectedness, the secrets we keep, and the pain that comes from a hard stare at the truths about ourselves.

With *Animal,* we launch Studio X, a purposefully eclectic constellation of innovative projects produced outside of our Main Series. Part of the inspiration for Studio X comes from four years of 'Lab' productions—plays that we developed annually, with writers in residence for much or all of the rehearsal process.

We present *Animal* as part of the Women's Voices Theater Festival, an unprecedented effort by almost all of DC's theatre companies to highlight the vibrancy of DC theatre, its growing enthusiasm for producing new work, and the American theatre's embarrassing track record of producing far too few plays written by women. Studio is proud to participate, and to offer to the world this potent play that reminds us how easy it is in our culture to write a woman off as 'crazy.'

I'm happy to have you among this play's first audience and hope you can feel the thrill that comes from seeing the creation of something new and unique.

David Muse
Artistic Director
The Studio Theatre

Dramaturg's Perspective

"Have you ever seen an animal bewildered? It's horrific."

"I'm interested in stories that go untold, in plays that can shine a light on a very dark place," Clare Lizzimore says, and her work is unafraid to put its characters in peril. Lizzimore's first play, *Mint*, followed a man's alienation and attempts to acclimatize to a changing family during and after his seven-year incarceration. Written in short scenes with language that is both direct and evocative, the play offered a perceptive and unflinching portrait of one family's turmoil, shame, and fury.

With *Animal*, Lizzimore turns her empathy and ravenous imagination to mental illness. There's a mystery in the heart of the play—a dark and unknown abyss that the main character, Rachel, circles around. I won't disclose the play's secrets here, but Lizzimore has drawn on an actual psychiatric condition to inform the play's narrative and structure, which mirrors the disorienting experience of a chaotic mind. Rachel is haunted by…something, a presence or event or absence that's been robbing her of sleep, resilience, and eventually, hope. Armed with a sense of humor and arresting propensity for cruelty (alongside its reliable kickback of self-loathing), she tries to reconstruct her past from available clues—slivers of remembered information, evidence of behavior she can't recall, night terrors that point to a darkness she cannot name.

Following the leaps and elisions of a mind in disarray, *Animal* alternates between torrents of language, tense scenes of crossed connections, and stretches of anxious stillness as Rachel ricochets from conversations with a husband who struggles to remain understanding, a therapist she charms more than cooperates with, and an intruder with whom she has an uncanny connection. Lizzimore draws on imagery both clinical and primal to fill out Rachel's world, taking on the language of nightmare, folk tale, and pharmaceutical banalities. Animated by Lizzimore's unsentimental curiosity, *Animal* offers a fearless look at the vulnerability and resilience of our animal bodies and expansive minds, each capable of their own breathtaking acts of cloaking and restoration.

Adrien-Alice Hansel
Literary Director
Studio Theatre

Playwright's Biography

Clare Lizzimore is a playwright and an Olivier-Award winning director. Her first play, *Mint* (2013), was produced at the Royal Court's Open Court Season and long-listed for the prestigious Bruntwood Prize. Her first radio play, *Missing in Action*, was broadcast on BBC Radio 4 in 2014, her new radio play *The Rage* will be broadcast in 2016. She is currently under commission with the Royal Court Theatre and the Almeida Theatre.

As a director, she has worked extensively in new writing, and her latest production—*Bull* by Mike Bartlett—received the 2015 Olivier Award for Outstanding Achievement in An Affiliate Theatre for its production at The Young Vic; it premiered at Sheffield Theatres and also toured to 59E59 in New York. Other recent directing credits include *One Day When We Were Young* by Nick Payne in the Roundabout Season at Paines Plough at Sheffield Theatres and Shoreditch Town Hall; *Lay Down Your Cross* by Nick Payne and *On the Rocks* by Amy Rosenthal at Hampstead Theatre; *Pieces of Vincent* by David Watson at Arcola Theatre; *Faces in the Crowd* by Leo Butler at the Royal Court Theatre; *War and Peace* and *Fear and Misery* by Mark Ravenhill at the Royal Court Theatre; *Jonah and Otto* by Robert Holman at the Royal Exchange Theatre; and *Tom Fool* by Franz Xaver Kroetz at Glasgow Citizens Theatre and the Bush Theatre, which was nominated for four CATS Awards. Lizzimore's directing awards include the Channel 4 Theatre Directors Award and the Arts Foundation Theatre Directing Fellowship. She has been resident director at the Citizens Theatre, Glasgow, and a staff director at the Royal National Theatre.

Studio Theatre

Now in its sixth season under the leadership of Artistic Director David Muse, Studio Theatre is Washington's premiere venue for contemporary theatre, "where local audiences will find today's edgiest playwrights" (*Variety*). One of the most respected midsized theatres in the country, Studio Theatre produces the work of today's greatest writers, augmented by occasional productions of modern classics, performed by acclaimed actors in intimate spaces. Throughout the Theatre's 37-year history, the quality of its work has been recognized by sustained community support as well as with 329 nominations and 61 Helen Hayes Awards for excellence in professional theatre.

Animal premiered at Studio Theatre (David Muse, Artistic Director; Meridith Burkus, Managing Director) in September 2015.

It was directed by Gaye Taylor Upchurch with the following cast:

Rachel	Kate Eastwood Norris*
Tom	Cody Nickell*
Stephen	Joel David Santer*
Dan	Michael Kevin Darnall*
Older Woman	Rosemary Regan+
Little Girl	Anais Killian

and the following production staff:

Set Designer	Rachel Hauck
Costume Designer	Kathleen Gelard
Lighting Designer	Jesse Belsky
Sound Designer	Daniel Kluger
Dramaturg	Adrien-Alice Hansel
Fight Director	Jonathan Ezra Rubin
Production Stage Manager	Allie Roy*
Assistant Stage Manager	Christine Ruthenberg-Marshall
Production Manager	Josh Escajeda
Technical Director	Rob Shearin
Assistant Director	Paul Lysek

Opening Night: October 4, 2015.

Animal was generously underwritten by David and Jean Heilman Grier, with additional support by Albert Lauber and Craig Hoffman.

*Members Actors' Equity Association, The Union of Professional Actors and Stage Managers in the United States. + Equity Membership Candidate

Cast

Rachel. 40's.

Stephen. Rachel's psychiatrist. 30's.

Tom. Rachel's husband. 40's

Dan. A stranger. 20's.

A little girl.

An older woman.

A note on the text

A beat lasts as long as it takes to read the word beat.

A pause is slightly longer than a beat.

A dash — represents an interruption.

A backslash / represents the interruption point for two people interrupting each other.

Three dots...represents a deliberate stopping of one word or thought, to better phrase the next part of the sentence.

Words in brackets ( ) are words that are intended but the character never gets to say them.

Character names denoted underneath each other without a space indicate two characters talking at exactly the same time, like this:

> *Rachel* —
> *Tom* —

*Words in bold and italics i.e. **Take her**, are words that are shouted.*

NB
This publication went to press before opening night in Washington and may differ slightly from the play as performed. Please contact Casarotto Ramsay & Associates for the final script.

This play could not have been written without Mike Bartlett; Dr. Barbara Byers; Claire Chambers; Adrien-Alice Hansel; Dr. Chris Hilton, Consultant Psychiatrist; David Muse; Amy Rosenthal; Jon and NoraLee Sedmak; GT Upchurch; Simon Vinnicombe; and Dr. Justin Wakefield, Consultant Psychiatrist.

C.L.

PROLOGUE

(*A memory.*)

(*Very faint, distant piano music plays.*)

Tom   Your knees.

Rachel   Knees don't change.

Tom   Maybe I've just never noticed them before.

Rachel   Okay yeah I'll take that, you're right (*Laughs.*) I do /
              have good knees

Tom   Your fulcrum.

Rachel   That's a lever in a car.

Tom   Oh, yeah, I meant clavicle.

Rachel   What's that?

Tom   The bit that goes in, just there, above your heart, below
              your neck.

(*Beat.*)

Rachel   What if I change even more?

Tom   I'm expecting it.
Rachel   Forever. What if I get really fat?—

Tom   Then I'd love you all the same—

Rachel   What if my thoughts change?

Tom   What?

Rachel   What if my thoughts change?

Tom   Then good. That's what thoughts are supposed to do.

ONE

(*The lights snap up.*)

(*Rachel and Stephen are mid-session.*)

(*Two pens are in Stephen's pocket, a Parker and a plastic ballpoint.*)

Rachel   I take that on. I take that on board. I do. But. I find that… It's worse, actually if you say that, it's worse.

Stephen   There are many other people who / I

Rachel   I'm not expected to meet them am I? / Don't do that.

Stephen   No.

Rachel   I don't want to do that.
Stephen   You don't have to

Rachel   That's like putting someone with claustrophobia in a lift and saying it's okay because there's this whole other group of people who feel exactly the same; and don't worry they'll *all* be here in a minute.

     (*Beat.*)

So, you know what? Instead of meeting them—

Stephen   You don't have to meet / them

Rachel   I'm going to go / 'cause I said to Tom I'd come

Stephen   You— (don't)

Stephen   And that's good that you did
Rachel   And now I've come. And I think you've seen me.

     (*Beat.*)

And maybe you're magic 'cause I feel better. So all I need is the paper.

Stephen   What paper?

Rachel   The certificate / the thing.

Stephen   I can't—

Rachel	I'll take that now please to give to Tom, and to work, and we can just all go back normal. Yes you can. You can sign a thing, and you can tick a box.

(*Beat.*)

Stephen	I can.
Rachel	Yeah right so—
Stephen	But I need to ask you some questions first.
Rachel	You've done / that.
Stephen	Not all of them.

(*Pause.*)

I need to know if, over the past two weeks, you've felt little pleasure or interest in doing things that you usually enjoy? On a scale of not at all, some days, many days, or every day, Rachel, what would you say?

Rachel	A questionnaire?
Stephen	It's not a questionnaire.
Rachel	It sounds like a questionnaire.
Stephen	It's not as simple/ as—
Rachel	You think you can put a number on it?
Stephen	You can. We do. It helps.
Rachel	What am I scoring so far?
Stephen	Six.
Rachel	What's crazy?
Stephen	Twenty-seven.
Rachel	How many questions?
Stephen	Nine in total.
Rachel	What if I lie?

Stephen   Try not to.

Rachel   Will you know?

Stephen   Whom will you help if you do?

     (*Pause.*)

Rachel   You know what's really surprising to me.

Stephen   What's surprising?

Rachel   That there's a business here. In what you do.

     (*Beat.*)

Stephen   That's what you feel.

Rachel   Yeah. That's what I feel.

     (*Beat.*)

     'Cause, everyone's on Xanax, on Prozac, aren't they. The drug companies must be loaded / and I'm not saying that 'cause I'm jealous.

Stephen   The drug company's—

Rachel   I'm saying it 'cause it's not natural is it? All of us on this stuff, this stuff, this scaffolding?

Stephen   If you think of yourself like a house / and that house is damaged.

Rachel   I don't.

Stephen   You can't start with the roof. You've got to lay the foundations. And that's what the medication is for.

Rachel   (*She smiles.*) They gave you a pen.

Stephen   I'm—(a doctor)

Rachel   I know how it works. The reps, they come in. They say have a free pen. Then they say okay, "I'm here to talk to you about this drug, the latest drug, the drug it's all about." And what is it called? Turn your pen over. There it is. Branding. Bribing. You're all doing it.

Stephen   You feel upset that your symptoms, they're not unique.

Rachel   Do you have a pen?

Stephen   I'm a doctor Rachel. I need to write prescriptions.

(*Pause.*)

Rachel Will you write one for me?

(*Beat.*)

'Cause, I know I said what I said, but actually I think I qualify. Actually I think I want the king. I think I want the one you wheel out from the vault marked 'supremely fucking excellent'. 'Cause if basically everyone's on it. Then why aren't I?

Stephen   We need to do some assessments first.

Rachel   Please.

Stephen   We need to talk about what it is you feel is happening to you?

Rachel   If I took off all my clothes, painted myself cerise, and ran down the road, no one would bat an eyelid, would they?

Stephen   You've told me that you feel your symptoms aren't unique but you've not told me what they are?

Rachel   You know what they'd think? They'd think. Maybe it's a new craze. They'd think, maybe I should do that; paint myself red, yeah, that looks like fun. Not, that woman needs some help.

Stephen   I need to ask you some more questions. We need to look at other routes before we prescribe you any medication. Before we look at the possible dosage—

Rachel   We've flooded the market. Hiding in plain sight. All the mad, depressed, the angry. But people are smiling and putting it on the catwalks, and all the while, these people are screaming.

(*Beat.*)

And actually they're in the woods. They're lost in the woods. And they should be in hospital—

Stephen You want to be in a hospital?—

Rachel I want to rest.

Stephen You feel you can't rest at home?

Rachel Can you rest at home?

(*Beat.*)

I haven't been sleeping. I've been waking up in the middle of the night. Not just waking up, but waking myself up. There've been weeks. Whole weeks.

Stephen Are you having thoughts of hurting yourself, or harming anyone else around you?

Rachel That's quite a question?

Stephen It is.

Rachel That's question two?

Stephen No. That's question nine.

Rachel What happened to two through eight?

(*Beat.*)

Stephen I need your answer Rachel.

Rachel I don't want to sit, or lie down, or think. I want to do, and buy, and eat, and shop, and gather.

Stephen Is there any reason you feel— (you have to)

Rachel To get ready for the fucking storm up ahead.

(*Beat.*)

I went out. I went to a shop and it sold everything.

Stephen Which one? Tesco's? 'Cause everyone goes a bit mad in there. (*A small laugh.*)

(*Beat.*)

Rachel   Oh my God. Was that a joke?

Stephen   It was / a

Rachel   My God, you're trying to lighten the mood?

Stephen   No / I

Rachel   When did you graduate?

Stephen   It's important to see the funny side.

Rachel   That something you learnt?

Stephen   Draw a smiley face.

Rachel   Excuse me?

Stephen   Draw something that's troubling you. Then next to it. A circle, a circular smiley face.

Rachel   Really?

Stephen   Really.

Rachel   I didn't know I had to participate in my own therapy.

(*Beat.*)

Got a pen?

(*Stephen passes her a pen.*)
(*Rachel reads the name embossed on the pen.*)

Rachel   Effexor.

(*She looks at him, shakes her head.*)
(*Beat.*)

So. What? Go on? What's the game?

Stephen   It's not a game—

Rachel   It's a game—

Stephen   It's an exercise.

Rachel	I've got to think about something that's troubling me.
Stephen	Yes.
Rachel	Only one?
Stephen	Start small. And draw it. And next to it a smiley face.
Rachel	That's it?
Stephen	That's it. Here. Have some—
Rachel	I'll do it on my hand.
Stephen	Don't do it on your hand that's—
Rachel	I'm doing it. Okay. It's drawn.
Stephen	So. Now look at it.

(*She looks.*)

How do you feel about the drawing? The thing that was troubling you? With the smiley face next to it. Doesn't it all seem a little *less* troubling?

Rachel	It seems…
Stephen	It makes you smile. Doesn't it?
Rachel	A bit yes I suppose it does.
Stephen	You deflate the importance of the troublesome thing. You resuscitate your sense of humour. This is just a little exercise, it's silly and simple, but it might help you to understand that there are principles we need to work on that aren't silly, in fact they're very important. Like looking after yourself; washing and eating, we'll start with the basic, fundamental things— Have you eaten today?
Rachel	I had breakfast.
Stephen	What did you have?
Rachel	Six cups of coffee, and some speed. (*Beat.*) That's a joke. C'mon, I'm resuscitating my sense of humour.

Stephen	That's good.
Rachel	That's not the ideal response to a joke is it?
Stephen	What's the ideal response?
Rachel	Well, to laugh, I suppose.

(*Beat.*)

Stephen	Rachel. You didn't answer my question before. It's important to be honest. Are you having thoughts of hurting yourself, or harming anyone else around you?
Rachel	No. No, I'm not.
Stephen	Your husband was anxious / that.
Rachel	Yeah.
Stephen	But you don't want to harm yourself.
Rachel	No.

(*Beat.*)

Stephen	Many people / who
Rachel	Don't start that again.
Stephen	Okay. Okay.

(*Beat.*)

Some people who I see feel as anxious—

Rachel	I don't feel anxious.
Stephen	Who feel as low—
Rachel	I'm not low.
Stephen	Who are as distressed as you are Rachel, may also have other experiences that trouble them, I wonder if I can ask you a few questions / to see
Rachel	What experiences?
Stephen	Hearing voices, feeling paranoid, withdrawal, ideas / of

Rachel   No.

Stephen   These are just routine questions, okay?

Rachel   Okay. Yeah. No.

Stephen   No.

Rachel   Yeah. No.

　　　　(*Beat.*)

Stephen   The ultimate aim is for you to be able to stand in the middle of a storm, be buffeted on every side by the world, but remain centered.

　　　　(*Beat.*)

　　　　Are you still cooking—

Rachel   Do you ask men that question?

Stephen   Yes, it's not a gendered question.

Rachel   Yeah. / I'm doing that.

Stephen   Not just for yourself.

　　　　(*Beat.*)

　　　　Okay that's good. That's really good.

Rachel   Is it?

Stephen   It is, but I want you to come back and see me in a few days. We can monitor your progress. You can book at the front desk.

Rachel   I don't get my paper?

Stephen   No.
Rachel   My certificate?

Stephen   There's not really a thing, a paper, a proof. You can technically go back to work whenever you want. You don't need a certificate for that. It's your decision. But I'm not recommending it. There's no reason to rush, to put yourself in a position of greater stress.

Rachel   But that's up to me.

Stephen   Technically, yes. But I wouldn't / recommend it.

Rachel   Recommend it.

Stephen   That's right.

(*Beat.*)

I want you to take your time.

(*Beat.*)

Why don't you try, tonight, doing something nice for yourself? Something for you.

(*Beat.*)

Rachel   Like what?

Stephen   Have a think.

Rachel   I can't think of anything.

(*Beat.*)

Stephen   Anything you want? Something comforting.

(*Beat.*)

Rachel   I'm finding this a bit upsetting.

(*Beat.*)

It's hard to think of something just for me.

Stephen   What about a face pack / a masque—

Rachel   What?

Stephen   A masque a / treatment—

Rachel   Oh so you mean, put some bubbles in the bath? Dress in a white robe, little white peep toe slippers, and a face masque, and think of smiley things?

Stephen   Your choice. As I say, something nice to / treat yourself—

Rachel   You want to know something they didn't teach you at school? They didn't teach you that it's women in the movies that do that, and that real women step in shit on way home, and spend the journey doing scrape-y sideways walking to try and ditch the stench. But. Inevitably. It gets stuck in the grooves and you're actually, with all that shuffling, you're grinding it into the soles.

(*Beat.*)

And then, you know what happens then? Your bags split as you're crossing the threshold, so your shopping's all rolling about in the dirt as your kicking it in the house, with those shoes, the ones with the shit. And then you get in (*Tiny beat.*) and there's a power cut. So you eat your dinner in the dark, after cleaning your shoes in the sink, and they're there on the counter sodden and fucked up with the memory of shit and you think, at least the shoe has its double.

(*Beat.*)

So now they're sat there, stinking, but smug, smug 'cause there's two. And you're just one. Until your husband comes home. And even then, laying there in the dark, the shoes have it better. 'Cause at least they're a match.

(*Beat.*)

Where do you buy face packs? Tesco's. Now there's an irony.

TWO

(*A memory.*)

(*Very faint, distant piano music plays.*)

Rachel   Do you ever have those days where you hear some music, see a man doing a back flip in the park, an artist sketching. And it takes your breath away. And you think, stupidly you think, I can do that, I can do all of that, if I just picked up that violin, or that paintbrush, or ran wildly into that jump, by some miracle I'd be able to do it. Without any practice or training, suddenly I'd be able to do it *all*. I had that thought today.

(*Beat.*)

You bought into something here.

Tom   I did.

Rachel   And you have to live with the consequences.

Tom   I am.

THREE

(The lights snap up.)
(Tom and Rachel.)
(Kitchen.)
(Rachel is exhausted and much more lethargic than we've seen her. She is only just able to engage, but she's trying.)
(An Older Woman is sat in a wheelchair drinking milk from a beaker.)

Tom   He was looking right at me.

Rachel   Okay.

Tom   Delaying going upstairs to the meeting/ Yeah— And asking me.

Rachel   He (was)?

Tom   It was lucky I / had an answer ready to go.

Rachel   You show your books?

Tom   No.

Rachel   Right.

Tom   Don't look like that. Don't look like that. You've got to play it slow with him. / It's a bit of a leap

(Rachel sighs.)

from 'what do you think?' / To 'I've solved the whole concept and these are my drawings'.

Rachel   It's not so big.

(Beat)

She lost the...she needs help with the...

(Tom sorts out the beaker and puts it more steadily in the Older Woman's hands.)

Tom   I'm just saying it was good I had an answer ready to go.

Rachel   So what did he say?

Tom	Well. The phone rang so—
Rachel	Yeah—
Tom	Yeah, I was trying to answer him, I was telling him. I wasn't sure what to do? What would you have done? Pick up the phone and / waste the opportunity?
Rachel	Yeah, no.
Tom	I fucked it didn't I? Did I fuck it? (*About the Older Woman*) Ah. Sorry. Sorry. Sorry to swear. It just. I had to speak quite fast, and the phone was ringing, it was loud, fucking phone, you know? Sorry. But he was smiling and nodding and I think, I hope, he heard me.
Rachel	He didn't.
Tom	What?
Rachel	He didn't hear you.

(*Beat.*)

(*Tom laughs under his breath.*)

(*Beat*)

Tom	Thanks. Thanks very much.

(*Beat*)

Rachel	It's true.

(*Long Pause.*)

Tom	It was a mark of respect. For being good, and kind and…I would have answered him. I could have answered him.

(*Long Pause.*)

I even checked my breath after, he was that close, patting me on my back. Hard, you know. (*He makes a back-slapping noise.*) Like that. (*He makes a back-slapping noise.*) It's the first time I thought thank God we're open plan. You should've seen Gary, jealousy in motion. Had his tongue hanging out his mouth, like a dog out the window of a car... I'm definitely not just a secretary to him now, am I? That's what Gary was thinking, I could see it.

(*Pause.*)

Can you stop looking away?

Rachel	I'm looking at what I'm eating.
Tom	But you could look at us occasionally too.
Rachel	Sure.
Tom	What, we irritate you?
Rachel	Actually yes. I don't like the way you jiggle her about. It's confusing. You want her to drink. You want her to laugh. You want her to—
Tom	She's fine. She's happy.
Rachel	How can you tell.
Tom	I can tell.
Rachel	You never spend any time with her.
Tom	Yeah so right, so when we're together you can at least look at me.
Rachel	Why?
Tom	Because I want you to talk with me, engage with me, I've asked you how it went today / and you won't tell me, so—

(*Rachel starts to cry.*)

Don't cry. Why are you crying? Don't you think? / Talking to each other?

Rachel	No.
Tom	So what? Sit in Silence? / Or talk about our day?—
Rachel	Yeah.

Tom	Our individual experience, of the world, what we've done. What we've achieved.
Rachel	(*She recovers.*) *Achieved?* I achieved not defecating on your clothes, but in hindsight maybe that was an error.
Tom	Don't do that—
Rachel	Don't look at me / like you hate me—
Tom	Lash out / don't do that—
Rachel	I achieved / not burning the house down—
Tom	I just want you, to tell me the truth.
Rachel	So I suppose I achieved sustaining a human life. And that's a big thing. That's a big big thing.

(*Beat.*)

But mostly, I achieved getting out of bed, Tom.

(*Pause.*)

Tom	But you talked to him?

(*Pause.*)

You didn't cancel did you, 'cause if you cancelled / then that's really bad.

Rachel	Wait.
Tom	I want you to look at me, so we can—
Rachel	*Wait*
Tom	What?
Rachel	Just. Stop.
Tom	Why are you closing your eyes?
Rachel	I'm drawing.
Tom	What does that mean?
Rachel	You know what *drawing* is.

Tom	I don't understand.
Rachel	In my mind, I'm drawing you.
Tom	If this is a game, then you should explain the rules.
Rachel	And I'm drawing your face, and your legs.

There are no rules Tom.

(*Beat.*)

There.

Tom	You've finished.
Rachel	I have. I've drawn your face. And it's smiling / A big stick man smile from ear to ear.
Tom	Well that's nice. My stick man self is smiling.
Rachel	Yeah. No. It's no good. I'm taking the drawing and I'm wringing the paper, like I'm wringing your neck, and I'm smashing you into the bin.

(*Beat.*)

I know you're having lots of fun at the moment. / And I should be trying to be fun too to compete with the fun, that you're having elsewhere.

Tom	It's work. **It's work,** I'm not—
Rachel	But I'm just so tired.
Tom	I know.
Rachel	No you absolutely don't. I got this.

(*Rachel takes out the facemask.*) It's supposed to make me feel better. I was going to do it after dinner. But I think that's too late. I think (*She rips it open and slathers it all over her face.*) I think I need it now.

(*She sits, and starts to eat again.*)

(*Beat.*)

(*Tom sits. He's mortified. But doesn't want to show it for her sake.*)

(*Rachel eats.*)

(*Tom watches. This can take some time. He's struggling with what the right thing to do is. It's imperceptible.*)

(*Beat.*)

(*He leaves. He takes the Older Woman with him.*)

Tom   (*To the Older Woman.*) Come on. Let's go and watch some TV.

(*Beat.*)

Rachel   (*Shouts after them.*) She shouldn't watch telly after 6 or she turns into a…

(*She rubs her eyes. We can hear the sound of the TV from the next room.*)

That stings. Ouch.

(*She closes her eyes.*)

Ow. Ow. Ow. Typical. Shit. Great. Shit. Tom. Tom!

(*Beat.*)

I can't open my eyes. Can you hear me?

(*Beat.*)

Tom?

(*Beat.*)

(*She laughs.*)

Great. Brilliant. Just my fucking luck.

(*Beat.*)

Okay. Fine. I'll just wait. I can wait. I'll just wait.

(*Beat.*)

I'll just wait.

(*Beat.*)

(*A young man enters the room.*)

Thank God. I can't open my eyes. They really sting. It really hurts. Fucking Tesco's. (*She laughs.*) I was just going to feel my way along the walls, to the bathroom and wash it off. But it's really weird. Have you tried walking with your eyes closed lately? I suppose not. Why would you? Well I can tell you, don't try it, it's fucked up. What's she watching by the way? Sounds loud. She'll get all worked up before bed, particularly if it's *The Antiques Road Show*, she wants all the things, keeps pointing, demanding, and I'm not dealing with it.— Why aren't you speaking to me?— Okay look. I'm sorry about before. I can be cruel and dark, and I know I'm hurting you. But I love you. I do. It's both. It's not a binary thing.

(*Beat.*)

What's she watching? I'm sorry about before. I can be cruel and dark, and I know I'm hurting you. But I love you. I do. It's both. It's not a binary thing.

(*Beat.*)

It's good about your boss. It really is. I just don't want to see your face when he promotes Gary and not you, 'cause he will you know, he just will. You don't see it. But they're ruthless, they're sharks, and they're big fat cats and they don't care at all— Like when he doesn't acknowledge you in the lift, borrows your pen and doesn't return it. And the sleepless nights with the worry, and just knowing he doesn't worry about you.

(*Beat.*)

I went.

(*Beat.*)

Says he doesn't need to see me again. Clean bill of health. I'm out of the woods. Said, me in the shop that was just normal, normal levels of anxiety, just normal.

(*Beat.*)

You in here? Or—

(*Beat.*)

Did you hear what I said? I can't open my eyes or they'll sting, I tried and it hurts. I might be allergic. Ironically it's the most un-relaxing thing I have ever done. (*She laughs.*) I can't think of anything worse to be honest.

(*Beat.*)

Talk to me.

(*The Young Man goes to Rachel, close, and kisses her.*)
(*She kisses him.*)
(*He holds his hands over her eyes and kisses her again.*)
(*Rachel leans into the kiss a bit.*)

Rachel	I could
Dan	I know.

(*Rachel suddenly realises it's not Tom and struggles free.*)

Rachel   Urrrrrrr. Ahhhhh. Ahhhhh. Stay away. Keep away.

Dan   I know.

Rachel   Oh my God this is—

Dan   I know.
Rachel   You kissed me?!

Dan   I know—

Rachel   Stop saying I know. What are you a psychopath? Don't answer that.

Dan   This stuff smells great.

Rachel   What if I hadn't opened my eyes?—

Dan   Mango?

Rachel   We could've / that's serious.

Dan   Or apricot? Have you a got a towel?

Rachel   I mean it, breaking and entering is one thing but—
              (rape)

>   (*Beat.*)

>   What you've done is serious. My eyes hurt, and my
>   heart's a bit… But I know you're not going to kill me /
>   Are you?—

Dan   No.

Rachel   No. 'Cause you'd have done that already wouldn't
              you? If you were going to kill me. You would have
              already done it / wouldn't you?

Dan   Yes.

Rachel   Well then. That's. Good. That's— My husband is just
              in there and he's massive. Huge. I mean it. I'd leave
              now before he comes and—

Dan   But you can deal with me on your own can't you?

Rachel   Yes. Yes.

Dan   I like you.

Rachel   *What?*

Dan   You're a good kisser / you're soft, sexy, I like your
              tongue.

Rachel   You should leave now.

Dan   You need to get Yale locks. And a door bar, steel rod,
              runs straight down the seal. That's the only thing we
              can't break through. Out of interest. I wouldn't have
              harmed you. I mean I won't. Do you want a cigarette?

Rachel   No. *Yes.* But not from you, 'cause you, I think you
              should / leave my house now.

>   (*Dan takes his T-shirt off, he wipes his face.*)

Dan   My name's Dan. By the way.

Rachel   OK. Dan.

(Dan offers her his T-shirt.)

Dan   You want it?

Rachel   No.

Dan   I think you do.

(She takes it and wipes her face.)

Dan   I like maths, and mechanics. / Forensics.

Rachel   Ok. Am I allowed to say I don't care?—

Dan   The small. The detail. Of things.

(Beat.)

Rachel   Here

(She offers him back the T-shirt.)

     Oh my God, you're a child.

Dan   No.

Rachel   How old are you?

(Dan puts his T-shirt back on.)

Dan   I break in. That's what I do. Can get in anywhere. That's my challenge. To see how it's done. Then I feed it back. Give the pitfalls, loopholes, and then they…It's a service. I run a…It's how I get paid. Usually. For the knowledge, the in-side—

Rachel   Are you asking me for money?

Dan   Yeah.

Rachel   You're asking me for money?
Dan   You could pay me in another kiss if you'd like.

Rachel   You're green. By the way. You've still got all that shit on your face. You should wipe it better.

Dan   You like me.

Rachel   I don't.

Dan   You do. It's chemical. We work.

Rachel   How do you know?

Dan   I know.

(*Beat.*)

Dan   It's instinct. Animal. Pheromones I think they call them. A lust. You smelt me.

Rachel   I think you should, actually get out now. I could report you to the police. This is not acceptable.

Dan   You liked it. It's a feeling.

Rachel   I'm not having this conversation with you.

Dan   It is.

Rachel   Leave my house now.

Dan   But you kissed me?

Rachel   Under false pretenses.

Dan   You liked it.

Rachel   No.

Dan   Just admit it. And I'll leave.

Rachel   I didn't know it was you.

Dan   Doesn't matter if you did or didn't. You leant into me.

Rachel   I didn't lean.

Dan   You liked it. I felt it. It was new. You were surprised. You leant into me. You did.

(*Beat.*)

Okay. Miss…

Rachel   Mrs.

Dan   Okay. Mrs. I'll invoice you. I'll pop round tomorrow. Or you could just kiss me now?

Rachel   *Get out.*

Dan   That can only mean one thing.

Rachel   What?

Dan   That you want to see me again tomorrow?

(*He smiles.*)

FOUR

(*A memory.*)

(*Very faint, distant piano music plays.*)

Tom I'm going to sleep in the lounge.

Rachel Yeah, well, you should.

Tom I got five hours last night—

Rachel Lucky you.

Tom It's not a competition.

Rachel We used to list our favourite things about each other. You liked my knees.

Tom Yeah well, now I don't, 'cause all you do is fidget and kick me.

Rachel We never kiss anymore.

Tom What?

Rachel I've got a new one for the list. Philtrum. It's the indent under your nose. It's not symmetrical, you know that? In the womb the two sides of your face develop independently of one another and then at some point, before birth, they join in the middle. I looked it up.

Tom I'm asleep Rachel.

(*Beat.*)

I'm sleeping. I'm sleepwalking to the sofa.

(*Beat.*)

Rachel Your face didn't fuse properly. I've been thinking about it. Biology. Inheritance—

FIVE

(*The lights snap up.*)
(*Rachel and Stephen.*)
(*In Stephen's Office.*)

Rachel   I was given a penny. In a box. When she came back
with us. Supposed to be lucky or something. I thought.
Thanks. We're going to need it. Tom was delighted.
Everyone under one roof. Triumphant. I just thought.
Where's the amphetamines, where's the MDMA,
where's the… anything…ibuprofen. (*Tiny beat.*) Now
I'm just a carer. (*Tiny beat.*) He loves his mother. I
hated mine. He's better. Why doesn't he do it? (*Tiny
beat.*) So then I'm crying at counters, weeping into the
arms of the checkout girls, not 'cause I'm sad, or
depressed or—'cause I hate myself.

   (*Beat.*)

Stephen   Have you heard about circadian rhythms Rachel? That
our body is informed by light and dark—

Rachel   What do you mean light and dark?

Stephen   It's not a metaphor. It's actual.
Rachel   Yeah I feel one and not the other.

Stephen   How affected we are by light. Daylight. If you don't
get enough good quality sleep at nighttime, it can lead
to more than just tiredness. Do you have curtains, in
your bedroom?

Rachel   I essentially just told you I want to kill my mother-in-
law, and you're talking about haberdashery.

Stephen   On a scale of one to ten—

Rachel   Every day I'm worse.

   (*Beat.*)

   You've seen Tom, haven't you?

Stephen   We had a session yes.

Rachel   I told him you didn't want to see me again. That I was better.

Stephen   You lied.

Rachel   Yeah. But I forgot you were doing follow-ups. So. Busted.

(*Beat.*)

I've aged him / by decades.

Stephen   No one is to blame.

Rachel   Haven't I?

(*Beat.*)

I need a cigarette.

(*Beat.*)

Are you getting this?

Stephen   I am.

Rachel   But you're not writing. Where's your pen?

Stephen   I'd prefer to listen, rather than write. It means I can pay you the fullest attention.

Rachel   That sounds very practical.

Stephen   It is.

Rachel   I'd give you enormous stone tablets if I could, get you to carve it in, to prove forever that someone actually heard, once.

(*Pause.*)

Although, sadly, I think anyone would listen, actually, if you paid them.

(*Beat.*)

If I were a stranger and we were out, and there was a bar and I was sat there, and I said, I begged you, I begged, 'Please would you write this down. Write down what I'm saying, because this way I'll know it's not all…that someone is…that you…you're *really…*'

(*Beat.*)

Would you do it?

(*Beat.*)

(*Stephen gets his pen.*)

(*Beat.*)

Stephen   I'd like to know how you've been since we last met, Rachel.

Rachel   But you know from him.

Stephen   There's a lot he can't know. He can see, he can assess, care, but he can't know.

Rachel   And you can?

Stephen   If you don't mind me saying, you're a little more unsettled today, a little more manic / maybe?

Rachel   Manic?

Stephen   Yes.

Rachel   Are you allowed to say that?

Stephen   A bit more excitable, excited, maybe?

Rachel   I tried out your thing.

(*Beat.*)

I was having an argument with Tom. Did he tell you? I drew him in my head, and it wasn't that fun or funny to be honest, neither of us were smiling.

(*Beat.*)

He was a bit.

(*Beat.*)

He looked sad.

(Beat.)

Like I was lost to him.

Stephen　*(Pause.)*

Rachel　You know you go on mute when you do that, don't you? Like there's a button on a remote control and I accidentally sat on it.

(Beat.)

That, or you're having a stroke or something.

(Beat.)

Don't write that. Please don't write that. Okay.

(Beat.)

(She gets up; she puts on her coat during the following.)

You know what. I've broken it / I've been cruel—

Stephen　It's not broken,

Rachel　and there's an atmosphere / now—

Stephen　There isn't an atmosphere. I promise. You've brought up some images, and topics that I'd like to—

Rachel　Your pen still has a lid on, I noticed that last time. Not your plastic ballpoint the one you got from the medical reps, but the shiny silver one. That one. In your pocket. It has a lid. And your briefcase closes.

Stephen　Yes.

Rachel　Not lying open stuffed to capacity at your side. But closed. Upright. Like a General.

Stephen　And why do you find that significant?

Rachel　The other doctors, I see them, when they're running, busy—whole lives play out in that waiting room you know? I see them on their way in, eating their lunch walking, their briefcases full of yesterday's case-files and old sandwiches. But there's order here.

Stephen   Do you equate that with naivety?

Rachel   I think you don't have a lot of files in your bag. Maybe that's a good thing. Maybe when you get more experienced, you get more jaded.

Stephen   You think order can't exit alongside wisdom?

Rachel   I very much doubt what wisdom is? When it comes to this? Don't you think?

(*Beat.*)

I brought back the penny, in its box. And I looked at it for a really long time. And I remembered that when I was little my mum took me to a place, with a tower.

(*Beat.*)

She said it would be an adventure, and it was. We climbed all the way to the top, it was so high up there and cold, we leant over the edge and she looked like magic, with frost on her hair, and she said 'look', and she brought out a penny.

(*Beat.*)

"This penny, this shiny, tiny, penny here in my hand, its harmless, look," and she hid it behind her ear, she made it do a little dance, she let me touch it and trace the man's nose, but then she said, throw it over the edge, let nature do its work, let gravity hit its metal sides, and its lethal. This penny given the right circumstance can kill.

(*Beat.*)

I'm worried I'm the penny. Doctor. (*Tiny beat.*) I found this. On my phone, and I don't know what it means. I can't remember if I've heard it before and forgotten? Or…

(*She plays the message on the mobile, it's from Tom, he's raging.*)

Tom　　　　"Do you think this is game? ***Do you think this is a
　　　　　　　fucking game?*** Where are you? Where the fuck are
　　　　　　　you? You left her, you just fucking left her. I just told
　　　　　　　you to get out, to go out the house; it's not my fault.
　　　　　　　I'm calling someone. And you're going to meet them.
　　　　　　　And you're going to sort this out."

Stephen　　Why don't you sit down?

　　　　(*Beat.*)

　　　　What do you think it means?

　　　　(*Beat.*)

　　　　Your husband sounds cross with you.

　　　　(*She stays standing but gets out a packet of cigarettes.*)

Rachel　　Mind if I smoke? (*She lights up, and takes a puff. Tiny
　　　　　　　beat.*)

　　　　I know you do, by the way. I know it's against the
　　　　rules. This is a medical building, so it's probably even
　　　　illegal.

　　　　But it's definitely in some code you have. Isn't it? So
　　　　what I can't work out is, why you let me? You're an
　　　　anarchist. It's the only logical conclusion. You get off
　　　　on it, illicit— You writing that down?

　　　　(*Beat.*)

　　　　What's there to write?

　　　　(*Beat.*)

　　　　'She smokes.'

　　　　(*Beat.*)

　　　　Femme fatal. Isn't it? Doesn't it? Imply?

　　　　(*Beat.*)

　　　　Imagine. They used to say smoking was good for your
　　　　health like apples. That's why I don't eat apples, 'cause

one day they're just gonna do a 180 and go "oh yeah you know that 'apple a day keeps the doctor away' thing, well turns out the doctor's a cunt, and apples give you cancer". (*Beat.*) So I'm just going to keep smoking. At least I know what I'm going to get.

(*Beat.*)

Good scribbling.

(*Beat.*)

You doing short hand? My grandma did short hand. All those lines and dashes standing in for words and meaning. She was clever. Were people better back then? Do you think? People. Just generally.

You're just letting me speak. But there's a plan. Isn't there? Tell me there's a plan.

(*Beat.*)

I might just have another / cig

(*Stephen removes the cigarettes.*)

Stephen   Why don't we put these over here?

Rachel   Why? You want one?

(*She smiles at her own joke.*)

(*Pause.*)

(*She decides to stay; she takes off her coat, but doesn't sit.*)

Stephen   Would you like to take your hat off too?

Rachel   Why?

Stephen   Because, I'm wondering what's wrong with your hair?

Rachel   Nothing.

Stephen   Then why the hat?

Rachel   What's wrong with my hat?

Stephen   You were wearing it last time.

Rachel	Yes.
Stephen	You never took it off.
Rachel	No.
Stephen	How long have you been wearing it?
Rachel	Is that important?
Stephen	It might be.
Rachel	It's just a hat.
Stephen	When we last spoke, you said, it started in a shop. Were you wearing it then?
Rachel	Yes. No. I don't know.
Stephen	You said you'd been shopping. That day. You'd been in a shop. It was a very big open space. You gave the impression it sold everything—
Rachel	It did.

Electrics, food, photos, and animals, right there, creatures, real, living, breathing, rabbits, cats, dogs, iguanas. I mean it, and there were these fish, these fish who were launching themselves at the passersby, like they'd evolved somehow. One of them literally flew out of the barrel, the, what do you call it?

Stephen	Tank.
Rachel	Yes. That was the moment…where…

(*Beat.*)

He flew out of the tank into the air, and landed right on top of the make-up counter. Flapping and splashing in the blusher, so he's pureeing the dust and the more it flaps the more it's sinking in this gooey-pink quicksand. And he's panicked. And bewildered. Have you ever seen an animal bewildered? It's horrific. It knows it's dying. And it's looking at me. It's looking right at me.

(*Beat.*)

Stephen   That sounds horrible. It must have really frightened you.

Rachel   It didn't frighten me. Don't you see? It stared right at me. Accusing me. Like it knew me.

Stephen   It's easy to identify with something in pain, in peril—

Rachel   No. I'm saying. It channelled something essential, some weird-shit truth about struggle—

Stephen   It must be very confusing, and very disturbing, to feel sad / and in pain like the fish.

Rachel   Sad? He was fucking dying. He wasn't sad. He was exhausted. He was tired of a world that punishes you for wanting more, and drowning you when you dare to think outside of the…tank.

Stephen   I think your story is very real, and very powerful. It must be very difficult to have identified with this image of a fish, trapped in a tank, not content going round and round anymore, but propelled.

Rachel   Yes.

(*Beat.*)

Stephen   I want to talk about your hat.

Rachel   You do?

Stephen   Yes.

Rachel   My hat?

Stephen   Yes.

Rachel   You don't think the fish is? I don't know, remarkable, in some way?

Stephen   I think it made a big impact on you yes.

Rachel   But you'd prefer to talk about the hat?

central theme = male suppression of female expression —

Animal   35

Stephen   Yes.

Rachel   What about my hat, do you find, significant?

Stephen   Well. Why don't you try not wearing it next time, and we'll go from there.

SIX

(*A memory.*)

(*Very faint, distant piano music plays.*)

Tom   "Do you think this is game? ***Do you think this is a fucking game?*** Where are you? Where the fuck are you? You left her, you just fucking left her. I just told you to get out, to go out the house; it's not my fault. I'm calling someone. And you're going to meet them. And you're going to sort this out."

Rachel constantly commanded by others

Mentall illness represents breaking social norms (?), and opposition to her expression of her pain = enforcement of (gendered) social norms

SEVEN

(*The lights snap up.*)
(*Kitchen.*)
(*Rachel is finessing a proposal / lecture, putting on high heels, makeup, sorting papers all at once, and all in the wrong order.*)
(*She's busy, in a rush throughout.*)

Dan   You're beautiful.

Rachel   I'm concentrating.

Dan   I'll just watch you then.

(*Pause.*)

Rachel   This can't be interesting to you?

(*Pause.*)

I mean it. I've got a job to do. In fact I've got a million. I'm not joking. After this I've got nine hundred and ninety-nine thousand, nine hundred and ninety-nine to go, and I'm late. I'm going to be late. So I'm not entertaining you.

Dan   You're an Amazonian.

Rachel   Do you even know what that means?

Dan   Yeah.

Rachel   It means strong and muscular and— Did you actually mean old?

Dan   No. I meant sort of wise.

Rachel   (*She laughs.*) Wise? You have no idea. Wise isn't letting you in. Letting you in means I'm an adulteress.

Dan   It was just a kiss.

Rachel   I didn't mean to my husband, I meant to my psychiatrist. I haven't told him.

Dan   You don't need him. You're better. You're going back to work. Look at you. You look great.

Rachel	I do.
Dan	You're looking forward to it.
Rachel	What if I've been away too long?
Dan	You're trained for this.
Rachel	You're right.
Dan	Got qualifications.
Rachel	What if I need him. If it gets too much.
Dan	I'll do it.
Rachel	What will you say?
Dan	You'll call me.
Rachel	Yeah.
Dan	And I'll say…I'll say—does he have an accent?
Rachel	It's posh.
Dan	I'll say "you're lonely. And I'm excellent."
Rachel	(*Laughs.*) That's your diagnosis.
Dan	Any good?
Rachel	It's quite accurate actually.
Dan	What about me?
Rachel	You?
Dan	Do mine.
Rachel	I think. I think you cut your hair.
Dan	Yeah.
Rachel	Why?
Dan	'Cause I like you. So. I made an effort.
Rachel	You did that for me?
Dan	Yeah.

Rachel   You look good.

(*Beat.*)

Youth. No one tells you how much you'll miss it when it's gone. Well they do. But you don't listen you're too busy being young.

(*Beat.*)

You look nice.

(*Beat.*)

I don't know why I talk to you.

Dan   'Cause you can talk about stuff that embarrasses you.

Rachel   You know why people don't talk about stuff that embarrasses them?

Dan   'Cause it's embarrassing?

Rachel   So they can block it out. Create a different history.

Dan   That why you keep letting me in? So you can tell the truth to someone who doesn't really matter.

Rachel   I let you in, 'cause you'd get in anyway / right?

Dan   I would.

(*Beat.*)

Want a cigarette?

(*Rachel takes one.*)

Rachel   Just one.

(*She lights it, inhales.*)

I should stop this. But it's a release you know.

(*She unzips her workbag; she exhales the smoke into it and re-zips it.*)

[handwritten: → Actual expressions/ relief must be kept secret]

	That's sick. Isn't it? But my husband doesn't know I smoke.
Dan	He does.
Rachel	Why would you say that?
Dan	'Cause you stink and this place is a dump.
Rachel	Hey that's rude that's really rude. It's my home.
Dan	Yeah, but it's going to the dogs, you know that don't you?
Rachel	No.
Dan	Just admit it.

(*Beat.*)

Rachel	It's going to the dogs, but I don't know if the dogs would take it. They'd sniff it, and walk away. Like it's rotten. Disconcerting. Like something's hiding in the walls. And it's lurking there saying, what if you've made all the wrong choices?
Dan	But a lick of makeup, nice new shoes, walk out that door and shut it out.
Rachel	What do you mean?
Dan	You're going to fuck things up today.
Rachel	That's cruel. You know I'm nervous so you skewer me, right where it hurts.
Dan	People like you shouldn't have children.
Rachel	Where is this coming from?
Dan	Yeah, I feel that, women like you shouldn't have children at all really.
Rachel	Well that's good 'cause I don't.
Dan	Vacillating. So quickly. Morally vacant—

(*Rachel slaps him.*)

	Violence never taught anyone anything.
Rachel	I may look tired and up against it, but when I want to be, I'm magic. So I'm going to work today. No matter what you say. I'm going. <u>And I'm scared but that's good, exhilarating, and free, all the things I should feel</u> as a working… as a worker. <u>And when I get back home tonight, you are not going to be here.</u>
Dan	If you throw me out, I'll just break back in and hide in your walls, like you said, and you'd feel it, you'd think it, but you'd never really know.
Rachel	Go ahead, you do that, you play your silly games, but I've got a job to do, and you're wasting my time.
Dan	You kissed me.
Rachel	I don't owe you anything. It was a kiss. Grow up.
Dan	That's it?
Rachel	Yeah. That's it. Bye-bye.
Dan	Just dismiss me?
Rachel	Yes.
Dan	Just like that.
Rachel	Yes. Go. *Go. Go.*
Dan	Come on. I was just playing with you. You're my friend. We're friends.
Rachel	No, it doesn't look like we are.
Dan	(*Laughs.*) So entitled aren't you. It's astonishing. I mean it isn't. But it is. Like. What if I, I'll just slum it with this guy today, for fun.

(*Beat.*)

But then at night, I don't want to think about him. Don't want the idea of him getting in so it's locks and bolts. And scented candles. Fairy lights.

(*Beat.*)

Does it make you feel better? Cos I can get in anywhere.

Rachel Are you threatening me?

Dan I feel sorry for you. Because. The problem you're facing is that despite everything I have a grandeur—

Rachel (*Laughs.*) You've got to be kidding—

Dan A spark of greatness / charisma.

Rachel Ok. Look. Just. Sit down. Ok. You're scaring me.
Dan I'm going to be a master. You know, Kung Fu. It doesn't actually mean Kung Fu, I looked it up. It's actually like a thing. It means to master something. To be a master in. You could have a Kung Fu in being a bitch, if you're really good at it like you? Or a Kung Fu in pottery. Or bakery. And I don't know in what yet. But I'm going to get my Kung Fu. So I've got power. And I don't need to be patronized. Be kept around as a charge. A bit of raw life blood for a middle-aged, bored—

Rachel Say wife. Go on. Say it? Say it and I will claw off your face. I'm not looking for comment. For judgment. Not from you. Not from you.

Dan Why? 'Cause I'm just / *just*

Rachel Yeah. You're *just*—

(*He grabs her head.*)

Dan *NO.* I'm so much more. I've been waking up in the middle of the night lately, not just waking up, but waking *myself* up. Screaming like those women you see on TV in grief, at the road side, a dead child in their arms. Animal. Reptilian. Horrible. And you know what? I started to pray. To a God. Anyone that's up there. To say hear me. Hear me now. I've gone a long

Dan = personification of desires / emotions / insecurities that Rachel must repress way to prove that I don't need anybody. Right? But now. Right now. I do.

Older
Woman   *Maaaa. Maaaaa.*

Dan   Jesus.

(*He lets Rachel go.*)

What the hell is that?

Rachel   Oh God.

Dan   What is it Rachel?

Older
Woman   *Aaaa. Maaaaa.*

Rachel   I thought she was asleep—

Dan   Who—

Rachel   —she's supposed to be in bed—

Dan   Fuck sake. Is there someone else here?

Rachel   Maybe she'll go back down.

Older
Woman   *Ahhh ahhhh.*

Rachel   I better get her. She can't walk.

(*She leaves and comes back on immediately with the Older Woman in a wheelchair.*)

Dan   She's shivering.

Rachel   Well she shouldn't be. It's not cold.

Dan   She lives here?

Rachel   Yeah.

Dan   Where do you keep her?

Rachel	"Keep her"? I don't keep her anywhere. She's got her own room, through there. She's been ill since about December. Same cold. Just won't go.
Dan	I thought we were alone.
Rachel	Yeah well—
Dan	Scared the shit out of me.

(*The Older Woman tries to grab Rachel.*)

Rachel	What are you… Stop it. Are you cold? You better put a jumper on.

You want a jumper?

Dan	Can she hear you?
Rachel	Yes. Yeah she can.

You want a jumper?

(*Rachel opens a cupboard and takes out a jumper.*)

Dan	Is she alright?
Rachel	I don't know. Here. Take this one.

(*She places the jumper on her lap.*)
(*The Older Woman looks at it.*)

Put it on.

(*The Older Woman drops / throws the jumper.*)

Rachel	Don't throw it. If you don't like it, give it back.

(*The Older Woman looks at it more closely.*)

(*To Dan.*) She drives me mad.

Dan	Does she speak?
Rachel	To herself sometimes, but no not really…it's hard.

(*The Older Woman starts making a noise to herself.*)

For God's sake. Do I have to do everything?

(*Beat.*)

>Okay. Okay. Here. Give me your arm. One. Where's your hand gone?

(*She pulls it through the armhole.*)

>Oh. There it is.

(*The Older Woman laughs.*)

>Give me your other one. Two. Oh. Where's your hand gone?

(*She pulls it through the armhole.*)

>Oh. There it is.

(*Beat.*)

>No? Okay. Hand number two wasn't funny?

>Well. I tried. And you're warm now. So. That's good.

Dan Shall we go out then, we could go for a walk.

Rachel We can't.

Dan What?

Rachel We can't leave her.

Dan You mean you can't ever leave without—

(*The Older Woman tries to get Rachel's attention.*)

Rachel (*To the Older Woman.*) What?!

(*The Older Woman starts trying to take off the jumper.*)

Rachel Please just stop it—

>(*To Dan.*) She could come with us?

>(*To the Older Woman.*) STOP! I could hit you sometimes.

>(*To Dan.*) Sorry. I don't mean it.

Dan Okay let's take her then—

Rachel   Yeah but I actually think she's tired.

Dan   She doesn't look tired.

Rachel   (*To Older Woman.*) If you don't sleep now, you'll get irritable. Whining all day. Do weird things. Do you want to go to bed?

(*The Older Woman slaps her.*)

—

(*The Older Woman slaps her.*)

—

(*The Older Woman slaps her.*)

It's a universe of two. And I'm not moving. (*To Dan.*) You should go—

(*The Older Woman slaps her.*)

Dan   You should stop her doing that.

Rachel   For once please let there not be a fight, a fuss / a tantrum.

(*The Older Woman slaps her.*)

You can provoke me as much as you want. But I'm not rising to your bait.

(*The Older Woman slaps her.*)

You can be a real bitch, do you know that?

Dan   Can I help?

Rachel   How?

Dan   I don't know…

Rachel   I'm drowning.

(*The Older Woman points to a cupboard.*)

You've eaten. You've already eaten.

(*To Dan.*) She has.

Dan   Yeah.

Rachel   What do you want? This?

(*She holds up a can.*)

No. Okay.

This?

(*She holds up a can.*)

Heinz. Okay Heinz. But you had your lunch. I gave you lunch. And technically, you're still supposed to be asleep. But you want soup. For some reason today. You want Heinz soup. Alright. You win. You win because I don't care anymore. Okay? You win. But it's full of sugar. And you can't have sugar. Or you'll die. Or something. Soon as possible I hope. But you want Heinz soup, so you'll have it.

Dan   Where's your husband? / Doesn't he help?

Rachel   But then it's straight back to bed. No fussing.

**Older
Women**   You hate me.

(*A moment. They look at the Older Woman—.*)

Dan   I thought you said—

Rachel   Yeah. Well maybe she does talk sometimes. I don't know.

(*Rachel tips the soup roughly into a bowl, puts a spoon in it and puts it on the table.*)

There.

(*The Older Woman tries it. Doesn't like it. Picks up the bowl and starts spilling it everywhere. .*)

Christ sake.

(*The Older Woman throws her spoon.*)

(*Rachel picks it up—gives it back.*)

(*The Older Woman throws her spoon.*)

(*Rachel picks it up—gives it back.*)

(*The Older Woman throws her spoon.*)

(*Rachel picks up the spoon and force feeds her. Aggressively. All of it. Spoon by spoon as she struggles. This goes on for quite a while.*)

Rachel You spiteful. Spoilt. Spoilt. Spoilt.

(*Rachel stops. Looks at the Older Woman, who's upset and worried. At Dan, who's standing at the back of the room, just watching.*)

Sorry. I tried to hide her from you. I'm so so sorry. Oh my God.

(*Beat.*)

I don't know what I'm doing. I'm sorry. I don't know what I'm doing.

(*Rachel cries.*)

Dan You're covered in it.

Rachel What?

Dan Red.

Rachel Oh no no no no no.

(*The Older Woman starts trying to take off her trousers.*)

(*Pause.*)

Dan I should go.

Rachel Yeah.

(*He does. Rachel picks up the Older Woman's trousers.*)

You need help?

Come on.

Come on then. You need a change? Are you wet? You want these off?

(*Tom comes in.*)

Tom   She okay? / What's going on?

Rachel   Yeah. Yes. I didn't hear you. You just got back?

Tom   She been wet for long?

Rachel   I don't know Tom. I didn't time it. I don't have a buzzer and a stop- watch. Don't judge me. It's not that bad. / Don't stand there and judge me.

Tom   Isn't it?

Rachel   You come in. You've not been here and you don't see that for the rest of day, we paint, press flowers / do baking.

Tom   What happened with the soup?

Rachel   What does it look like?

Tom   Armageddon.

(*Beat.*)

Why are you dressed for work?

↳ Older woman = represent-
ative of Rachel's maternal/
spousal responsibilities

EIGHT

(*Many memories.*)
(*Very faint, distant piano music plays.*)

Stephen	Think of something nice.
Rachel	Okay.
Older Woman	maaaa
Tom	Do you think this is game?—
Older Woman	Maaa
Tom	*Do you think this is a fucking game?*—
Stephen	It's a key moment—
Older Woman	*Maaa*
Rachel	How many particles in space?
Tom	I'm calling someone.—
Dan	Ten
Stephen	There's a view that this state you find yourself in is just a legitimate response to the world.
Older Woman	*Maaa*
Dan	I hadn't finished—ten quadrillion—
Stephen	When a baby learns to operate—
Dan	Ten quadrillion, vigintillion—
Older Woman	*Maa*
Stephen	to experience the world, it will find that it's dangerous, but predictable in that danger.

Tom	…You're going to sort this out.
Stephen	and through that discovery, it's managing.
Older Woman	*Maaa*
Rachel	Tom?
Older Woman	*Maaa*
Stephen	You're managing, too—
Dan	One-hundred thousand quadrillion vigintillion atoms.
Stephen	You're managing the world.

NINE

(The lights snap up.)
(A park.)
(Rachel, Older Woman, and Tom.)

Tom   I brought your wallet and your keys.

Rachel   I left them behind.

Tom   Which is why—

Rachel   On purpose.

Tom   But you haven't even brought her food with you.

Rachel   She doesn't need to eat all the time.

Tom   And if she got hungry, you wouldn't have had the money to buy her anything.

Rachel   We'd have gone feral.

Tom   This isn't a joke. Come on, what's happening here? It's 7 o'clock in the morning.

Rachel   She woke up early.

Tom   Why are you wearing those?

Rachel   'Cause they're comfortable. Loads of people are wearing them.

Tom   Yes 'cause they're running / they didn't

Rachel   So, I'll run in / them

Tom   wear them in bed last night.

Rachel   How do you know?

Tom   They put them on to exercise this morning. Not to sleep last night.

(Beat.)

You're basically wearing your pajamas.

(*Beat.*)

Do I need to call him?

Rachel   —

Tom   It's seven in the morning. I wake up. You're not there. Nor is she. Your wallet's on the counter so are your keys. What am I supposed to think?

Rachel   That you sleep too long, you'll lose your family.

Tom   You're punishing me for sleeping?

Rachel   How did you find me?

Tom   There's only one park.

Rachel   I could've gone to a café?

Tom   The cafés don't have accessibility for—

Rachel   My life is that predictable. I walk out on you and like a bad smell I can't lose you.

Tom   Is that what you're doing?

Rachel   I don't know Tom, why don't you work it out for yourself.

Tom   Is she okay?

Rachel   She's great. It's an adventure. My mum took me on them all the time.

Tom   I brought her hat. You left her hat.

(*To Older Women, putting her hat on.*) Here you go. That's better.

Rachel   She was fine.

Tom   It's bright sunlight, and its high in the sky, so I don't want her head to burn.

Rachel   She was fine. You're fine aren't you?

Older Woman	Ma-Ma.

(*Rachel laughs.*)

Tom	Why are you laughing?
Rachel	She keeps calling for Ma-Ma.
Tom	Why is that funny?
Rachel	It's just silly. Look at her. She's calling for her Mummy. (*To Older Woman.*) Your mummy died a long time ago.
Tom	Don't say that. That's a wicked thing to say.
Rachel	It's true.
Tom	I'm calling the police.
Rachel	Why, I didn't kill her.
Tom	Are you coming home with me, or not?
Rachel	You're all about calling in other people to do your dirty work aren't you?
Tom	If I need to.
Rachel	Is that a threat? Why are you escalating this? It's ridiculous. Like what? I've abducted her? It's a walk in the park.
Tom	I need to know that she's okay.
Rachel	She's excellent. She had tomato soup for lunch, dinner and breakfast. She's buzzing. Come on let's just put her on the swings and then go home
Tom	She's not going on the swings.
Rachel	Why not? She loves them. It's like crack to her.
Tom	She's been on them before?
Rachel	Yeah loads of times.

Tom   But it's dangerous.

Rachel   Yeah, if you could die from having fun, yeah it's lethal.

Tom   I'm saying it's not sensible, I'm saying it's not right she's / too—

(*Rachel loses it.*)

Rachel   I look after her all the time. I know what she likes, and when she likes it. You want a say, then you do more. You clean her arse. You bathe her when she's wriggling and biting. You deal with her when she wakes up at 12, at 2, at 4, at 6. You make her meals every day and cut off the crusts, the bad bits, the pips, the rind. Or. Wait. No. You go to work. You leave. Every day. Get your coffee from the man in jazzy little coffee cart, pick up the paper, stroll in, while I'm struggling with the shit, and the tears. So tell me not to put her on the swings.

(*Beat.*)

Or call the police. Say my wife and I are having a conflict of interest. She came for a walk. She wants to use the swings. They'll say who's the responsible adult here and we'll say well, my wife is the main carer—

Tom   Who's currently having treatment for —

Rachel   *Take her.* Take her home then.

(*Beat.*)

Just take her home.

Racne's illness becomes Tom's weapon against her, a justification of her subordination

56   Clare Lizzimore

TEN

(A memory.)

(Very faint, distant piano music plays.)

(The sound of a heart monitor.)

Rachel   They haven't checked me for ages.

Tom   They'll check on the next shift.

Rachel   I can't—
Tom   Let's sing a song.

Rachel   What song? Fuck off. I'm not singing.

Tom   Three little men in a flying saucer, flew round the world one day, they looked left and right and they didn't like the sight so one man flew away—

Rachel   That's a hideous song. It's a bit existential. It's a bit dark. Actually. I think it's brilliant. How does it go?

ELEVEN

(*Night. Rachel and Tom in bed. The light is out*)
(*Rachel gasps.*)

Tom It's okay. It's okay. I'm here.

Rachel I'm scared.
Tom I know. I'm here.

Rachel You came back, from the / couch.

Tom I did. It's more comfortable it's like Siberia/ in there.

Rachel Don't joke / don't.

Tom Why? It's funny.

Rachel You won't sleep in here. I'm too noisy. You hate me. I kick you.
Tom It's okay. I don't care. I'm staying. I don't hate you.

Rachel Help me sleep. Please help me sleep. Don't let her come for me.
Tom Okay. Okay. It's okay. Shush. Shush. Shush. Shush. Shuuushh. Shuuush.

Tom Okay?
Rachel Okay.

Tom Do you think tomorrow, Rachel, we can talk in the light.

Rachel What do you mean in the light?

Tom I <u>mean in the day. Not just like animals in the dark,</u> <u>snatched moments, out of dreaming, between bed</u>—

Rachel We do talk in the day.

Tom I mean come out with me.

Rachel Okay / Okay.
Tom Okay?
Rachel Okay. Maybe.

Tom You're sure?

Rachel   I'll think about it.

Tom   A date.

(*Beat.*)

Rachel   Your feet. By the way.

Tom   Yeah? (*He laughs.*) My feet?

Rachel   Yeah. Your feet.

TWELVE

(*A dream.*)

(*Very faint, distant piano music plays.*)

Rachel   (*Singing.*) One little man in a flying saucer, flew round the world one day. He looked left and right / but he didn't like the sight—

Girl   (*Singing.*) but he didn't like the sight so one man flew away.

THIRTEEN

(*The lights snap up.*)
(*Stephen's office.*)

Stephen   Can you tell me what happened?

Rachel   I can draw it. If you want, I can draw it? But I can't say it.

Stephen   Well let me just.

(*His pen, which has been clipped to his white shirt, under his jacket, has leaked all over his pocket. He exhales in anger.*)

Rachel   Shafted.

Stephen   Excuse me?

Rachel   Turns out the pen's no good?

Stephen   Yes, it does seem so.

Rachel   Got a job to get that stain out now

Stephen   I do.

Rachel   Tissue?

Stephen   (*He smiles.*) No thank you. I'll just go and get myself cleaned up.

Rachel   I definitely won't look in your briefcase.

(*He smiles, and goes.*)

(*Rachel sits in his chair, she swings around, she picks up his briefcase, puts it on her lap, she gets out his pencil case and from it two erasers, or bits of blue tack, and two pens, she then sticks the pens in the erasers / blue tack, and performs the Charlie Chaplin routine from* Gold Rush, *where he makes forks stuck in bread rolls dance, like legs in shoes—She does it brilliantly. She packs it all away. And discovers a file.*)

(*She reads.*)

Rachel "Mrs. G is 43 years old, multi-medicated, and has been referred to me with...

(The lights flicker, she looks up, she looks back.)

She recently explained that she was 'terrified' to go to sleep because during a recurrent nightmare she was pursued by…

(The lights flicker she looks up, she looks back, the flights flicker she looks up, she looks back.)

As a result her anxiety has reached a level of vivid intensity…

(A ten-year-old girl appears)

You've missed my routine. It was very good— (it was)

(Rachel gasps.)

Girl Stained, I think. You'll see it there forever. Ingrained. My shirt may as well be blue. But it doesn't matter. You were doing some sort of a routine. May I see it?

Rachel I'd rather not no.

Girl I never normally leave. I'm sorry. I can see that it's upset you…You've found my notes.

Rachel Who's Mrs. G?

Girl How far did you get?

Rachel Vivid intensity.

Girl I see.

(Beat.)

Rachel Things seem to be going very badly with Mrs. G. Don't they?

(Beat.)

Girl My chair.

(They return to their own chairs, in their correct places.)

Thank you.

(*Pause.*)

Girl   What about the file, may I have it back too?

Rachel   I want to keep it.

Girl   Why don't we agree that you'll close the file. But you can keep it safe, while we talk. How about that?

(*Rachel closes the file. But keeps it with her.*)

You were going to draw me a picture, before, you were going to—

Rachel   Yes.

Girl   Would you still like to?

Rachel   I don't need to.

Girl   I see.

Rachel   What do you see?

Girl   I see you Rachel. What do you see?

Rachel   I see something that scares me.

Girl   What scares you?

Rachel   A little girl.

(*Beat.*)

Girl   I think there is something nameless—

Rachel   Is it religious?
Girl   A dread that these visions stand in for.

Rachel   Am I having a religious vision? Maybe you're me? Are you me as a child and I'm remembering something that's been blocked and hidden to me for all these years.

(*Beat.*)

Or maybe you're regret?

(*Beat.*)

Something wasted? All the while babies grow to girls, girls like you, and still I'm swimming. I'm stuck. And it's got to stop.

(*She starts to rip the folder fast, into little bits.*)

If you stand still for too long, you'll stay like that.

(*She rips. She stops. She's remembered something.*)

That's what my mum used to tell me.

(*Beat.*)

Oh my God. It was terrifying.

(*Beat.*)

Every night. Hearing about this man, this man who was very, very, fast. He's rushing around, has no time for anything meaningful—but something happens to him—I can't remember what, but after this...moment he goes the other way; he tries to push back, to burrow back in time. He really thinks about it. Breaks down the data. He starts to count everything, steps, mouthfuls, blinks—and with painstaking practice, he trains himself to go slow. He gets obsessive, resisting impulse, squashing reflex, and just on this slow burn, this pilot light, he just exists, living out of time, out of sync, in anti-gravity. He takes a month to eat breakfast. A year to blink. A decade to walk to the bottom of his garden.

(*Beat.*)

But by this point, he can't go back, he doesn't know how. He's lost the ability to speed things up. It's the point of no return and he's turning into this pale-eyed, wiry haired, *thing.*

(*Beat.*)

And the voice she used in the dark, it was terrifying, "And if you look hard enough you can still see him to this day, making his slow-slow journey through cornfields and countrysides, all the while lamenting, with his arms up to God, why he couldn't have learnt balance. Not too fast. Not too slow. Just right."

Girl   I see. It was a scarecrow.

Rachel   No. You don't, you don't see. The horror of it. What he's doing. Going back and forth, punishing himself, reconstructing actions, unpicking it all to find the precise moment where it all went wrong. You never see. No one ever does.

(*Beat.*)

Why?

(*Beat.*)

Why?

(*Beat.*)

What happened to his wife?

Obsessions = personal shame, a fear of time passing, and the feeling that her ("his wife's") own failings are the cause of this obsession

FOURTEEN

(*A memory.*)

(*Very faint, distant piano music plays.*)

Rachel	(*She laughs.*) It's a bit existential. It's a bit dark. Actually. I think it's brilliant. How does it go?
Tom	Three little men in a flying saucer
Rachel	Three little men in a flying saucer
Tom	Flew round the world one day.
Rachel	What if I can't handle it.
Tom	You can.
Rachel	Sometimes I can't. I'm changeable. Aren't I? I'm just saying you bought into / something here.
Tom	I did.
Rachel	And you have to live / with the consequences.
Tom	I am.

Tom is aware (maybe?) that they are playing roles, and Rachels sickness is the consequence

FIFTEEN

(*The lights snap up.*)
(*A restaurant. Rachel and Tom are drinking.*)

Rachel   That's. Wow. That's really—

Tom   Bestsellers apparently.

Rachel   You can tell you can tell.

Tom   You know it's 150 a bottle?

Rachel   We can't afford that.

Tom   I know.
Rachel   I mean we really… that's expensive.

Tom   I don't care, look.

(*He sips.*)

What's that? 10?

(*He takes a gulp.*)

30?

Rachel   Do you think most people do this all the time?

Tom   I don't care about most people. Tonight. It's you and me.

(*Beat.*)

Rachel   Thank you.

(*She smiles.*)

(*Beat.*)

Tom   I haven't seen you smile in so long. I feel like a student again.

Rachel   But this time round, you really know your wines!

Tom   I'm going to get another bottle. We've got a lot to—

Rachel   Let's save it / this is nice.

Tom	But we agreed.
Rachel	I'm here aren't I?
Tom	But I need you to talk to me I do I do I do I really—
Rachel	You're running out of patience. And I'm not getting better.
Tom	That's not what other people see. They see someone—
Rachel	No. I don't think they do.

(*Beat.*)

These things have consequences you know that don't you?

Tom	They don't. Not with a loving —
Rachel	I've been thinking of having a one-night stand. But that's vengeful. Isn't it? Not on you. On me. Revenge. 'Cause that's what they are, aren't they? They're punishments on yourself for getting everything else wrong.

(*Beat.*)

I could be doing this with him. But he's beautiful. And that's the only reason I can't. You should know that, that I don't want to *only* 'cause I'm old, and scarred, and embarrassed but,

(*She cries. Hard. Suddenly. No sound comes out.*)

I knew I'd do this. I promised myself. Hold it together.

Tom	I understand.
Rachel	*No.* Why are you so nice to me? You're banging your head against a brick wall here, and you just keep running, and there's blood, and it's in your eyes, but still you run, bang, bang, / bang—
Tom	'Cause I know you're behind it.
Rachel	What if I'm not?

Tom	Shall we…dance? Or something?
Rachel	Dance? No. No. This is why I didn't want to go out. 'Cause I knew you'd push me, to do things, to interact.
Tom	Just with me.
Rachel	I've just told you I've met someone else. That I was thinking of…and you want to dance with me?
Tom	Yes.
Rachel	Yes.
Tom	You've not done anything?
Rachel	No.
Tom	And you won't?
Rachel	No.
Tom	So good. So, I'm asking you to dance with me.
Rachel	You are.
Tom	Yeah.
Rachel	But there's no music.
Tom	Pick anything you want.
Rachel	Beethoven.
Tom	He scares me.
Rachel	He doesn't scare you, he intimidates you.
Tom	Same thing.
Rachel	You should have practiced more.
Tom	I should have done a lot of things.

(*He brings out a mini tape player from his bag.*)

Rachel	Oh my God, that thing's older than me.
Tom	Only just.

Rachel	(*She smiles.*) You went in the attic.
Tom	I did.
Rachel	You hate going in the attic.
Tom	I do.
Rachel	You can't play it here.
Tom	I can.
Rachel	People will look.
Tom	Let them.
Rachel	You just keep his sonatas in the player, do you, ready to go?
Tom	It was already in there. Which means you were the last to use it, so count yourself lucky 'cause it could have been Led Zeppelin.

(*She laughs.*)

Tom	Ready?
Rachel	No.

(*Tom presses play, it's a Beethoven sonata.*)

(*They dance. It's small. Intimate. Contained just by their private table. He leads. Brilliantly. She falls into it. Enjoying it. Being for a moment, elegant.*

(*Suddenly. Violently. She pulls away.*)

(*Tom stops the music.*)

Tom	What did I do?
Rachel	I can't.
Tom	That's okay.
Rachel	I hate you. / You can't help me. Not like this.
Tom	I know. I know. It's okay. We'll stop.

Rachel	Wait. *Let me put my head on your chest.* Before we go.
Tom	Okay.

(*She puts her head on his chest, and continues to stay like that in the embrace, throughout.*)

(*Pause.*)

Better?

Rachel	Yeah.
Tom	If I'd had known inciting a panic attack would make you cuddle me, I may have done it sooner.

(*She looks up at him, unsure, vulnerable.*)

Joke.

(*Beat.*)

Rachel	Tell me a story?
Tom	I don't know any.
Rachel	Make one up.
Tom	Your hair smells nice.

(*Beat.*)

Tom	Um…
Rachel	Ummmmmm. I like it when you do that. Vibrates in your chest. It's funny.
Tom	Stop it.
Rachel	Do it again.
Tom	Ummmmmmmmmmmmmm
Rachel	If suddenly. It overtook me. Completely. This. Black. This cloud. And it took me away forever. I want you to know. It's been really nice to know you Tom. To be married to you. Everything before. I liked that. I want you to know that. You wouldn't remember me as mad would you?
Tom	No, I wouldn't.

(*Pause.*)

Okay then. Ready to go home?

Rachel   I am.

(*Tom switches on the lights, to reveal that they are actually at home still, and have constructed the idea of a restaurant, and restaurant table, in their kitchen.*)

Tom   So that's it.

Rachel   It was good. You did a good job. It felt very real. And very authentic, and I think yes, next time, maybe, yes, we can go out.

Tom   Okay. That's good.

Rachel   I kissed him. The one I told you about.

Tom   —

Rachel   Did you hear me? I said. I kissed him. I did do something. I kissed him. I lied.

Tom   Ok

(*He sighs.*)

Rachel   You just sighed at me?

Tom   Yeah.

Rachel   That is almost the worst possible thing you could've done?

Tom   Is it?

Rachel   Sighed at me, like, what a loser? You know what. You deserve it. You deserve it all.

Tom   *I've done the worst possible thing, I have?*

Rachel   *Because that's just the fucking lowest form of side stepping shit for actually what could've been a really tasty set of expletives, for some really sexy fucking / language that actually—*

72   Clare Lizzimore

Tom	*Stop it. Stop it. Stop swearing.*
Rachel	What's wrong with me swearing? You swear.
Tom	No. Not like this. Not like that. You're a mess. You really really are. You push and push, and I put up with it. But no. Not now. Not this. I'm stopping you because I have to. Because someone / has to care.
Rachel	Right well good. Fine. And now you need to pass me that box.
Tom **Rachel**	But we're in the middle of— Yeah. Yeah. But I've been thinking about it, and I want to throw away the fairy lights.
Tom	Right now? We're finally talking and—
Rachel	Yeah, yeah, I think yeah. Right now.
Tom	Please. We were having a good night weren't we?
Rachel	Yeah.
Tom **Rachel**	So maybe we should just… No. No I think I want to at least sort them.
Tom	They're Christmas decorations. And they're not yours to throw away.
Rachel	What do you mean not mine. / They're mine.
Tom	I'm not going to stand by and let you ruin that too.
Rachel	It's already ruined. Its ugly and brutal and sticking LED lights on it all won't change it. You know. There was a survey done of preschool children. And they were asked. 'If you could make one wish for what you would really like to be when you grow up, what would it be?'
Tom	I know.
Rachel	You do?
Tom	We watched it together.

Rachel	So, this little girl, she said, / 'Beautiful.'
Tom	Beautiful.
Rachel	Yeah. That's what she said. That was her answer. Not politician or astronaut—
Tom	But she *was*. Beautiful. Can't you remember? We said. Wow. Imagine, if, one day, *she* looked like / that?
Rachel	Who? Doesn't matter. But it's horrific isn't it? To put that first, put beauty first?
Tom	I get up every morning thinking, praying it'll be better, for Edie.
	Don't you?

(*Lights flicker. Reset.*)

Rachel	Who? Wait. What did you say?

(*Lights flicker. Reset.*)

Tom	"I get up every morning thinking, praying it'll be better, for…Edie."
Rachel	Who's Edie.

(*Tom gets up. He goes out.*)

(*Lights flicker.*)

Rachel	What?

(*Pause.*)

Older Woman	Maa maa.

(*Rachel rolls her eyes.*)

Rachel	Stop calling for your mummy! I told you, your mum died a long time ago.
Older Woman	Maa Maa

(*The Older Woman's cries turn into the cry of a baby.*)

(*Rachel turns in the direction of the cry, as if hearing it properly for the first time.*)

(*Tom enters holding a baby in his arms.*)

Rachel What's that? Where's your mum?

Tom My mum?

Rachel She was crying again.

Tom Edie was crying.

Rachel What?

Tom Edie.

This is Edie.

Did you forget?

(*She looks at him, the horror, everything sinking in.*)

In the midst of illness, she forgets her maternal role

More of the obsessed woman as opposed to the stereotypical nature of femininity
(

SIXTEEN

(*A memory.*)

(*Very faint, distant piano music plays.*)

(*A baby is crying.*)

Rachel   Do you want to go to bed?

(*The baby gives a loud cry.*)

—

(*The baby gives a loud cry.*)

—

(*The baby gives a loud cry.*)

It's a universe of two. And I'm not moving.

(*The baby gives a loud cry.*)

For once please let there not be a fight, a fuss/ a tantrum.

(*The baby gives a loud cry.*)

You can provoke me as much as you want. But I'm not rising to your bait.

(*Pause. The baby is still crying.*)

You can be a real bitch, do you know that?

SEVENTEEN

(*Stephen's office*)
(*Rachel is enraged. Sat next to her is Tom, holding a baby.*)

Rachel   And you just let me talk. You knew. You knew and it's
         sick. To let me go on and on, entertain you, flirt with
         you even, such oblivion. You should have wrestled
         with me. Both of you. Shouted. Screamed like a a a
         God, with wrath, with power, said *wake up, wake up,*
         wake up.

         Put your hand in, right into the cloud, and grabbed me.

         You should have searched, risked everything, come to
         me, huddled in the nightmare, and dragged me out.
         You should have saved me. You could have got me
         out, you should have got me out, you should have told
         me.

Tom   We've got you now. We've always had you. You're
         safe here.

Rachel   *I'm not. No. You didn't have me. You did not.* My
         fucking hat. (*She rips off her hat.*) That's all you could
         talk about. I want to shove it into your throat. You let
         me tell you stories, when all the time the dark was a
         living, breathing thing.

         You should have sent me for brain scans. Put me
         through metal, through machines, checked, for a
         tumour, cut it out. Broken laws. Defied physics.
         Instead you left me. Like an animal.

Stephen Birth can feel like an abuse on the body.

Rachel   Yeah. Yeah. That's right. And you can say, it's
         dangerous and it's life and death / but I'm an animal.

Stephen It's a trauma. A trauma that can sometimes affect the
         brain.

Rachel   But why? Why?

Stephen There's no real understanding of the cause.

Rachel	Of course there's not. Of course there's not. 'Cause <u>only women suffer it, right?</u>
Stephen	Postnatal psychosis—
Rachel	Tell me we wouldn't know exactly what it was if he had it, if you had it! If your brain didn't defy you, and betray you, right after giving birth, right after the most extreme fucking moment of your life, when you need to hit the ground running, have your wits, and your mind and… Oh my God.
Stephen	It's important to know that it's not your fault. There are many other women who suffer, and have suffered, and who have recovered. After one month, six months, a year, but they recover.
Rachel	Why didn't you medicate me?
Stephen	We did.
Rachel	What?
Stephen	We did.
Rachel	No.
Stephen	There's a lot you don't remember.
Rachel	No shit. No fucking shit doctor.

    (*Beat*)

    (*To Tom*) Did I take them?

Tom	Yeah.
Rachel	No. No I—
Tom	I saw you. I was with you.
Rachel	Well, they didn't fucking work did they.

    (*Beat*)

    I didn't hurt her.

Tom	No.

    (*She starts to cry*)

Rachel   I fed her.

Tom   Yes.

    (*Beat*)

Rachel   Will she remember, that when she first needed me, I failed?

    (*Beat*)

Stephen   No.

    (*Beat.*)

Rachel   I think my scarecrow man had a scarecrow wife.

Stephen   Did he?

Rachel   Yeah. And I think they had a baby, who was made of the best and softest straw. And the scarecrow wife said, I don't know how to love this baby, fragile made of sticks. So she bought it a rose. But the scarecrow man said, what do you think that is? And she said. Love.

    (*Beat.*)

    But he said. That's not love scarecrow wife. Can't you think of anything better?

Tom   I never. I didn't make / you feel—

Rachel   *It was never there to begin with.*

    (*Beat.*)

    So she thought. Yes. Of course I can. So off she went, slowly making her way down the stairs, out the house, and down the garden. But I don't think she's ever coming home. 'Cause she's still looking for the thing.

Stephen   Looking for the thing.

Rachel   The thing that she can bring back and say there.

    (*Beat.*)

There. That's love. Right there. That's safety. That's
kindness. That's protection. That's a promise. A
promise little girl, that we don't have to live in shit,
that there's not disease, and plague and suffering, that
the rich don't just get richer, that they're not the only
ones who are safe. That you can be exactly what you
want to be. Promise. I brought you into a world that's
fair, and just, and equal.

(*Beat.*)

And she's wracking her brains out there. And all the
while the baby made of sticks and straw, she's
growing, she's tall, she's beautiful; she's a beautiful
straw-girl. And she's clever. She passed all her exams
at scarecrow school. And you know, she's the most
beautiful, beautiful, pianist. And sometimes when the
scarecrow wife is crawling like an animal, in the dirt,
on her hands and knees looking for the meaning of it
all.

(*Beat.*)

She thinks she can hear this sound, and it's so beautiful
that it makes her cry, and she doesn't know why. And
then it hits her, hard, hard, in the chest. The simple,
simple, truth. The thing. The very thing she was
looking for. And then she laughs. She laughs in anger.
And rage. And spite. But she's lost in the woods so no
one ever sees her. And her husband—he's looking in
all the wrong places. In the light. In the fields. In the
sun.

(*A slightly longer beat.*)

I saw her. The little girl. And others, other people who
weren't real. But she was the worst, the little girl. She
was the scariest—

(*She looks at the baby for the first time.*)

That she would grow up. (*Beat.*) And I'd miss it all.

(*Beat.*)

80   Clare Lizzimore

There was a man…who I think I kissed. An old woman. I saw you as the little girl.

Stephen   Do you see me like that now?

Rachel   No. It was only once.

Stephen   What about the old woman

Rachel   No. She's gone.

Stephen   And the man?

(*Rachel shakes her head.*)

(*Beat.*)

Alright.

(*Pause.*)

I'm glad you took off your hat.

Rachel   I could skewer out your eyes.

(*Beat.*)

Why? Why are you glad I took off my hat?

Stephen   You were dressing yourself as a patient.

Rachel   What, and all patients wear hats?

Stephen   Yes. Hats just like that. And loose-fitting clothes, T-shirts, old trainers. A uniform for illness.

Rachel   So I'm not a patient anymore?

Stephen   No. I think you're going to get better.

[handwritten margin note: The men seem to condescendingly blame her for her illness suggesting they had to sit through water and...]

EIGHTEEN

(*A memory.*)

(*Very faint, distant piano music plays.*)

Tom   She's beautiful.

You okay?

Can you see?

She's perfect. Isn't she?

(*Beat.*)

Edie.

(*Beat.*)

She's Edie.

Right?

This is her.

NINETEEN

(*Tom and Rachel's house.*)
(*A cot. Rachel approaches it. Rachel looks in the cot.*)
(*She hesitates, unsure of what to do.*)
(*She switches on a mobile that projects stars all around the room.*)
(*She folds some clothes.*)
(*She goes back to the cot.*)

Rachel   Okay. (*Beat.*) I have a terrible voice.

(*Beat.*)

This is so silly.

(*Beat.*)

(*She sings.*) Three little men in a (*She stops.*)

(*Beat.*)

(*She stifles a cry.*)

(*Beat.*)

(*She shakes her hands, she runs her hands over her face; she composes herself.*)

As if you didn't already know I'm shit at this.

(*Beat.*)

Okay.

(*Beat.*)

Three little men in a flying saucer flew round the world one day
They looked left and right but they didn't like the sight
So one man flew away.

(*Her hands are shaking. She's stopping herself crying; she pushes on.*)

Two little men in a flying saucer flew round the world one day
They looked left and right but they didn't like the sight

So one man flew away.

(*She drops the toy she's holding; she picks it up and puts it in her baby's cot.*)

(*She takes deep breaths; she's coping.*)

One little man in a flying saucer flew round the world one day
They looked left and right but they didn't like the sight.

(*Beat.*)

So one man flew away.

(*Beat.*)

(*She looks behind her, suddenly, she looks back; she's terrified.*)

(*Black out.*)

End.

This play acts as a criticism of the disregarding of womens mental struggles

Rachel worries that she's failed and that her life is worthless, but these worries are disregarded as delusions despite their being based in sanity

Director's Perspective

A version of these remarks were given at the first rehearsal of Animal *at Studio Theatre on August 31, 2015.*

Before I was approached to direct this play, I'd never before heard of post-partum psychosis.

I suppose it's no wonder. It's a disease that only affects women, and it is a disease that carries with it great shame. We've barely begun to find it acceptable to speak openly about post-partum depression. And that condition affects a staggering 15% of all new mothers and in turn, their families.

But considering that 5% of women suffering from post-partum psychosis kill themselves, and another 4% of women suffering from it kill their child or children, the greater shame is that we don't speak about it.

We live in a society that loves to call women crazy. It's an easy out. It's an off-the-cuff seemingly innocuous phrase that gets repeated over and over and over: She's crazy. It's also a phrase that is dismissive. Damning. Leaving the accused powerless. Leaving anyone who believes it unwilling to perhaps empathize or give her the benefit of the doubt.

But we are used to labeling women. It's a deep-seated habit. And it's a convenient way to dismiss half the population.

What better way to silence women's voices than to make us think that if we speak our truth and reveal our fears then we will be labeled—by both men and women— as hysterical.

But surely the antidote to a simple label is complexity. If women are allowed to tell their stories with all the diversity and complexity intact, then labels can begin to fall away. Because while it may be easy to dismiss a woman whose story you do not know, how can you push her aside if you've learned that actually, her behavior is borne of a serious condition and one that, through no fault of her own, she's never even heard of.

And therein lies the brilliance of *Animal*: Through a beautiful rendering of encounters that include deep questioning with a psychiatrist, a liaison with a hallucination, and a marriage that is being stretched to its limits, and finally through seeing a person recognize herself as a mother for the first time, Clare's deeply complex portrait of a woman makes it absolutely impossible to dismiss our heroine Rachel simply as crazy. As bitchy. As not worthy of our most serious consideration and our deepest empathy.

Bearing witness to Clare's rewriting process has been awe-inspiring. If we were to spend tonight reading each of Clare's last three drafts, you would understand how fearless she is about cutting scenes, adding characters, changing the structure of the play. And yet, through all that, she kept her eye on what she wanted the story to be: "It's an unfolding of a person's mind," she told me. That thought has driven our design process, and will continue to shape the staging of the play.

There are many things we don't know yet. I'm looking forward to a process of real discovery. What I do know is this: I love Clare's play for many reasons—its humor and wit, its bold theatricality, its interweaving of a narrative which we don't have a full picture of until the end—but I also love it politically. I love that it sheds light on yet another illness affecting women that is not often discussed. I love that it forces us all to engage with a woman who is not necessarily well-behaved or always even likeable. We get to see many sides of this woman—and that is still, sadly, a rare experience in storytelling. I also love it that we get to see a patient, struggling, imperfect but loving husband trying to make it work—another kind of character we don't often see.

And I deeply believe that it is in this way—through recounting one personal, complex story at a time—that we can change perception, we can move the needle one iota in the direction of becoming a truly egalitarian citizenry.

We live in a world in which women's stories are discounted daily. Even in the industry of theater—a place which prides itself on being progressive and open—we fail women's voices miserably.

I'm hugely proud to be a part of Women's Voices Theater Festival—the first enormous gesture of its kind to help right the balance—to help us inch towards parity. Knowing that we are one of 51 stagings of world premieres by women in an eight-week stretch of time here in DC is profoundly moving to me.

I love that Studio Theatre commissioned and is producing Clare's play—a play that fits hand in glove with the ideas behind Women's Voices Theater Festival because not only is it written by a woman, but because Clare has created a character whose story is underrepresented in our canon of literature.

We desperately need this array of women's voices being offered up into the world. And I'm thrilled to give particular attention to the profound and exciting voice of Clare Lizzimore—whose is a voice to be reckoned with. Thanks, Clare, for writing this play, and thanks, Studio, for bringing us all here together. I'm excited to begin.

Gaye Taylor Upchurch